MW00380178

Never Give Up

-I Didn't!

James H. Cobb

DEDICATION

I would like to dedicate this book of memories to my wonderful

Partner and the Love of my life, Necia---

And to Cathy, Jack, James, Elaina, Jack David, Amy,

Cindy and Jim.

Each member of my precious family continually motivates me

to

Never Give Up!

ACKNOWLEDGEMENT

Writing a book had never crossed my mind.

Then I was blessed to meet my wonderful Speech Therapist.

After listening to me tell her some of my life stories,

she started encouraging me to write them down. Then she

insisted that I write them all into a book. This is the result of

that strong encouragement and gentle persuasion that she gave

me. So, all of the credit for the creation of this book goes to my

sweet friend and therapist, Julia Loughmiller, MS, CCC-SLP.

Never Give Up! --- I Didn't!

By: James H. Cobb

Introduction

What does this title mean? What is this book about? Why did I write this book? You may even think this is a weird or funny title for a book but I am hoping that this little story of my life will inspire and encourage a few people to never give up. If my story helps someone – I believe that makes it a success. I would like to spend the next few pages telling you about my life experiences and the lessons they taught me about not giving up. The stories are not necessarily all in chronological order and this book does not contain all the stories of my life (whew – that is a relief, you say!) but I have shared some of the highlights that have been important to me and have taught me the meaning and value of perseverance in this life. If you are wondering, there are two sources for these stories – some of them come from my own personal memories and others are borrowed from my older family members who sat for hours around a wood burning fireplace talking and telling stories for many nights during my childhood. When I was a young boy, I loved sitting and listening to them as they told stories and I hope you will love doing the same as you read this book.

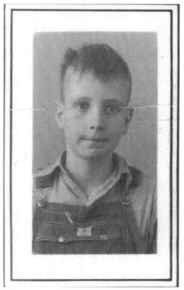

James Cobb in 2nd grade

Chapter One

In the Beginning – Stories from My Childhood

I was born March 15, 1932 in Athens, Alabama. Athens was a small, rural town of about 7,000 people in northern Alabama. This was during one of the worst depressions in our country's history. Very few people had any money because most folks didn't even have a job. The house my family was living in was a three-room house-- not a three-bedroom house. It was located in the poorest section of our town. We did not have gas, electricity, indoor plumbing or running water. We just had kerosene lamps for light and the only heat in the winter was a wood burning fireplace. In the kitchen, a wood burning cook stove was used for cooking.

There were eleven people living in the house when I was born. There was my grandfather and grandmother, my mother and father, two cousins, my two older brothers, one aunt and one uncle, and me. My parents, my brothers, and I moved a few months later to a house closer to town. My dad was fortunate to find a job with Limestone county. He was earning $25 a month as a heavy-duty equipment operator -- bulldozer and road grader. It was a time when no one had much money because jobs were scarce. My dad did not give up.

When I was three years old, I liked where we lived because we lived across the street from a family that had a young girl- she was probably a teenager. I liked her because when she and her mother would come over to visit my mother she would hold me in her lap. Also, that year she gave me the first Christmas present I had ever received. It was a toy dump truck filled with candy. One day my mother went out and left my older brothers to take care of me. I went to sleep and while I was sleeping my brothers ate all my candy. It really hurt me and I really got mad. In fact, I am still a little mad even if they are in Heaven with the Lord.

When I was five years old, we moved to the country. I often wondered how my father pulled off being able to afford housing for us on his limited income. We rented a very old house about three miles from town. The owner had a pasture across the road from the house and he let us keep our milk cow there. We also had a vegetable garden and a few apple trees. We still did not have electricity. We were living there in March, 1938 when I turned six years old. There were two types of schools in our area - the city schools that started in September and the county schools that did not start until two months later because the people who lived in the country had to pick the cotton crop in the fall. Regarding which of these schools I would attend, my mother and I made a decision during the summer before I started school that has affected my entire life.

When I was six years old, the first-grade teacher came out to our house during the summer and wanted to recruit me to come to the city schools. Since I had two older brothers going to the city schools it was a pretty easy change but we did have one problem to solve. During the first six weeks of the year, the first graders got out of school early – we would be out at noon. I solved this problem by agreeing to walk the six or seven blocks from the school to my grandmother's house every day after my half day of school. I was glad to do that because she always had the Sunday comics to read or she would take me to a movie where Tarzan was the hero. I did that for the entire six weeks. You may wonder where my grandmother got tickets for us to go to movies. As it was with most people at that time, she did not have any money. She used coupons she clipped off of bread wrappers that she bought and found. We usually got enough tickets for us to go to the movies two or three times a week. After all that time together, needless to say our relationship was very close until she passed away. She did not give up.

Another thing I learned to do when we lived in that house in the country was how to tell what time of day it was. My mother listened to all the soap operas on the radio. When a program came on, I would ask my mother what time it was. The names of some of these programs from my childhood were: Ma Perkins, Guiding Light, Stella Dallas, and Just Plain Bill. I did this so many times that when a program came on I automatically knew what time it was.

About this same time, my father got a new job with the company that built the Redstone Arsenal in Huntsville, Alabama, which was about thirty miles from Athens. The arsenal was providing supplies to our military-- Army and Navy. This arsenal eventually became the location where the U.S. Space Program started. My dad was employed as a heavy equipment operator and was building roads throughout the arsenal. That opportunity was an important life changing event for our family as it was the first good job my father ever had.

In December of my first-grade year, we moved again to a house which was in a neighborhood farther out into the country but close to very good schools. The place was East Limestone. Dad rented the house and it had a barn, pasture, and a well in the front yard. The pasture went into the woods. We all loved the house because it had just been built and we all had enough room. It had a little house in the back where we could keep meat if we salted and packed it right. We had two fruit trees in the back and two or three shade trees in the front yard. We moved in the middle of the year and that meant we had to change schools again. All of us, my two brothers and I, changed to a very good school. It had nine grades which meant all three of us could be in the same school. It was one half mile from where we lived so we could walk to school on nice days. There were 14 students in my first-grade class. One of the best things that happened at our new house was that my first sister was born on March 18, 1940. She was and still is an important part of the story of my life.

Sometimes there are memories that really stick with a person. One such memory happened in my class at school. There was a girl who sat in front of me and I did not like her. One day she came to school with an apple. She turned around in her seat and held the apple out and said, "Don't you wish you had an apple to eat?" I reached up and took the apple out of her hand and took a big bite out of it. She started crying and screaming. The teacher, Miss Balch, came back to me and marched me down to the Principal's Office. The principal took off his belt, took me out on the front porch of the school and gave me two strikes with his belt. When I got home, I told my mother about the spanking. She told my daddy about it and he gave me 3 strikes with a belt. I was a perfect student the rest of that year and if I was not, I made sure my parents did not know it. That was my personal rule all the way through high school that kept me out of trouble (for the most part).

A few people knew we were going to get into World War II, but not very many found out until the Japanese bombed Pearl Harbor on December 7, 1941. I was nine years old and I will never forget that day. We were at my other grandmother's house with some other people. I remember my aunt crying because her son was in the Army and she was afraid that he would have to go and fight. He never did but was killed by a jealous husband in a café somewhere in New Mexico not long after arriving there. I felt so sorry for my aunt. She was a widow and had no children.

1941: Luther, Joe Ann, Bob, James (9 years old) & Chuck Cobb
Five of the Eight Cobb Children

Chapter 2

Stories about School, Sports and Work

Our new school made sure that each class had some type of sports equipment. The most popular one was softball. They furnished a couple of balls and maybe one bat. I was in the first grade but played with the second grade because of my size. We played ball almost every recess and some mornings before school.

When I was in third grade, I received my first school award at the end of the year. In fact, I was the only student who received the very special award in all of the third grade — or in all of the school. I got the award for "perfect attendance for the school year," but the best part was that my teacher gave me a baseball bat for my prize. I was very excited!

Another thing that happened when we lived in East Limestone occurred when I was in the fourth grade - I got my first bicycle. This is the story: to make money, my mother was picking cotton, my oldest brother stayed home with my little sisters, Joe Ann and Sue, while my brother, Robert was the water boy and carried water to the cotton pickers. I told my mother I wanted to pick cotton so I could buy a bicycle. She asked me if I thought I could pick enough to buy a bicycle. I said that I did not know but I really wanted to try. She made me a bag that night and I picked cotton for about 4 days. At a penny a pound I knew I did not have enough money and it was a pretty miserable job. After working, I came into the house and I went to my room and shut the door. My mother came in and said, "I know how much you want a bicycle, so I will make you a deal. If you will stay out of trouble as long as you have the bicycle, then I will help you buy it." I was one happy boy! My father, mother, and I loaded up and went to town in my daddy's pickup truck to the hardware store and bought a bicycle. I did not give up!!!

There were a lot of happy days at East Limestone school but I have not kept up with everyone from those days. I do know that one classmate is still living. She is living in Athens and we call each other to set up class reunions. Her name is Mary Ann Meadows.

When I was in the fifth grade, we moved again around the Christmas holidays. My father found a house just outside the city limits of Athens. It was in the northwest section of the city which was a great section. He bought 10 acres. It had 4 acres of land that my father leased out, 4 acres of pasture and barn, 2 acres of garden and truck farming. The pasture was in the woods, so we all had a place to keep our animals and grow our food. It was a wonderful home.

When we moved, it was at a time in our country when building materials were rationed. You could not build a new house but you were allowed to add onto a house and that required a permit. There was a very small house on our new property which was not big enough for our family. So, dad told the contractor to add onto the old house, which was legal. The house was finished, and soon we found out that we could catch a bus to the city schools about one block from our house.

We started back to school after the Christmas break and our move and we did very well in the few months left. One thing I did notice at my new school was that the students did not play softball. They only played football and they played at all recesses. At first, I just watched. I watched a few games at recess until I could not sit still. I asked if I could play. After a few weeks my uncle drove by and parked and watched us play. Then he called my mother and told her that I was destined to be a star player. Of course, she had to tell me when I got home! He was my mother's brother and had played high school football.

Our second sister, Sue, was born on June 25,1942. Then only two years later it looked like the girls would soon start to outnumber the boys when my third sister was born in May 7, 1944 in a hospital in Athens. Her name was Linda and I was the older brother who was in the sixth grade. That meant that I helped care for three little sisters growing up. I learned how to change diapers, feed and dress them. I'm still very close to all three of the girls. Thinking about that experience has helped me not give up on several occasions.

During my sixth-grade year, our teacher received notice that her husband, who was in the Army was on his way home. It was a joyful ending to my sixth-grade experiences. Another exciting event happened - my teacher suggested that we select a captain of our football team and that someone would be me!

As my seventh grade approached, a Christian school with grades 7 through 12 was starting. My mother insisted that I go to the Christian school which was called North Alabama Bible School. There were several Churches of Christ in Limestone County (I think there still are). Most of the teachers, preachers, wives and a few other women rented a very old home to start the school. It grew enough to build several nice buildings and a very good school with grades 1-12. School met from July 15 to September 1. That would provide the children time to work in the cotton fields and do other things from September 1 to October 30. I realized that the students going to the Athens City Schools would lose their jobs when they returned to school in the fall. I heard of one job at the local garages that sounded good to me.

During this time a lot of things were rationed or not available at all. There were no new cars made or sold and auto parts were scarce, so the garages had to take the parts out that were bad. If those parts were usable, the garages hired someone to clean them with either water or gasoline. I wanted to be that person.

I got up one morning and went to the kitchen to eat breakfast. My mother asked why I was getting up so early. I said I was going to town. She said, "Why are you going to town?" and I said, "I am going to get a job." Silence! More silence! More silence!! Then she asked if I thought anyone would hire me. I said, "I will not know until I try!"

I walked to town and went to the garage. I walked into the garage and the owner came out of his office and asked me if he could help me. I said, "Yes sir." He asked what he could do for me. I said that I would like to have a job. His face turned pale and he looked at me like I had hit him. He finally asked why I wanted a job. I said, "I am tired of picking and chopping cotton and getting paid very little for it." I looked at his face when he turned around and I could see I had hit a nerve! He said, "I don't blame you at all!" and "Well son, when can you start?"

I answered him, "Right now, this afternoon or Monday morning." He said, "No we cannot do that. We have to order a Social Security card." I had no idea what that was. He said, "You have to have one. I think I can get you one by Monday morning. Come in Monday at 6:00 am." I thanked him and told him I would be there every day and do the best I could do. Before I left, I told him that I had a good bicycle with a basket to put the parts in. He told me that was great. Not bad for a 12-year-old seventh grader. I did not give up.

The next spring, one morning I was in the kitchen and Daddy came in and asked me if I had a job for the summer yet. I said, "No, not yet." He said that he had talked to Mr. Lunsford who owned a garage. My daddy traded with him. When Dad told him that I did not have a job, Mr. Lunsford told Dad to tell me I had a job as soon as I could get there. I did not give up!

I went to the Junior High School in Athens in the fall of the 8th grade. I transferred there because I wanted to play basketball. That was the beginning of another sport for me.

While all this was going on we got a new baby boy in our family on November 30, 1946. He turned out to be a great baseball player, a very good football player, and he ran track. He had the same football coach that I had. I believe that John and I are better men because we played for Coach Elmore. He was a fine man who really inspired both of us, and he always had our best interests at heart. In the spring of that year, I put together a baseball team. We played a lot and had a good team. The ninth graders and sophomores began to take over the team, so I quit playing and began to umpire. I umpired until school was out.

I transferred back to the North Alabama Bible School in the summer following my eighth-grade year because my mother wanted me to. I really did not mind because it opened up the jobs in the fall. After the summer I was happy to learn that Uncle Bill, the one that said I would be the athlete in the family when I was in the sixth grade, was holding a job for me. I went to see him, and he explained the job to me. He worked for the Dr. Pepper Bottling Company driving a truck and delivering soft drinks to stores in Athens, Decatur, and in Limestone County. The major product was Dr. Pepper with 3 other brands of soda pop. A lot of things were still rationed after the war. Soda pop was one of those because they used sugar to make the drinks and sugar was severely rationed. It was so bad that most restaurants and stores only got two cases of drinks twice a week. We would leave the plant every morning at 8:00 and return between 1:00 and 3:00 p.m. My job was to unload the truck every afternoon. To do that I had to take the empty bottles off of the truck and stack them so the people working in the plant could refill them. I enjoyed working for Uncle Bill at Dr. Pepper and signed on to work for another summer as well. During those years I also worked for a seed company – washing seeds and loading them into bags for delivery to the farmers.

Joe Ann, John, Linda and Sue with big brother James

At one time, I was hired to work for a company that was building a bridge across a river a few miles north of Athens. Although that was the best paying job I had, there was one problem. The man I was working with had a very foul mouth and bad temper. I tried to ignore him, but the day came that I could no longer handle it. He was wild. I threw my hammer down and started to walk off. I stopped and picked up my hammer. I was afraid that he would pick up the hammer up and throw it at me. I went to the office and told the two owners what had happened and told them I was leaving. They looked at each other and did not say anything for a few minutes. Finally, one of them said, "You cannot quit. We will give you someone else to work with, but you cannot quit!" They were hoping that I would go to Atlanta the next summer and work for them there. I stayed on the job for the summer but had to decline going to Atlanta because I knew my mother would not buy that. I will never forget those two men even if I cannot remember their names. They made me feel so good about myself!

I started playing tennis early every morning. I was playing when the coach put out the word that we would start meeting at the school at 10:00am for football. Well, I had started playing tennis at 8:00, then I would walk across the field to practice with the football players. One morning I was 10 minutes late and it made the coach so mad that I never missed a time or was ever late again. When it came time to put pads on, he named the starters. My name was not on the list. I had started the last 6 games last season, so it really hit me hard. My replacement was a senior who had never played in a game. I was shocked and disappointed. We won the first three games, but the fourth game was against a team that no one could remember the last time we had beaten them. We couldn't stop their running game. They were running around and over the senior tackle that replaced me. Coach Elmore signaled me to come sit with him. I went over, and he asked me if I could stop that offense. "I may not stop it, but I guarantee I can slow it down," I replied. The next thing I knew I had played 2 plays and made two tackles. When I came off the field, I looked over at the player that I had replaced and he was glaring at me - I would have been dead if looks could kill. But I didn't give up!

I did everything I could to help the team win but other than that one game, I did not get to play again during my junior year. I cheered for them, congratulated them for winning nine games and losing one. After the season, I tried my best to forget my disappointment and get ready for basketball. I played basketball that year but we did not have a good team and did not win many games. Looking back, it seemed like I did not do much except play ball and work.

After basketball was over, I began to wonder what I was going to do that summer about finding a job. Guess what? My oldest brother called me that afternoon and told me that Dr. Pepper had called him and offered him a job driving and delivering drinks. They told him that they wanted to hire me as his helper. It was an enjoyable summer because he let me drive a lot.

On two occasions a friend of mine, Oscar Barker, and I hitchhiked to Birmingham to watch the Alabama-Auburn football game. We went to see them play in 1948 and 1949. It was the first game that Alabama and Auburn had played since 1918. In 1948, we found tickets to the game and paid $14 for them. The score was 55 to 0 and Alabama won. In 1949, we were able to buy student tickets and only had to pay $2 each for the tickets. The score was 14-13, with Auburn winning. The only good part about that trip was that we ran into a friend who owned a shoe store. Both of us were his customers. He and his family rode the train to the game. He insisted that he buy us tickets on the train back home. We tried to pay for the tickets, but he would not take our money. That ride home was much better than having to hitchhike.

That fall our football team reported for practice and the team selected co-captains. Bobby Wood and James Cobb were selected, which was a great honor for me. I talked to one of our defensive ends from that team recently and he said we had only

22 players to report. He is still a good friend of mine, but I think he was wrong. I think we had 24 players. Coach Elmore, who is deceased now, was our head coach. I will rate Coach Elmore as one of the best coaches who coached me during all of my playing in high school and college. He taught me so many valuable lessons - life lessons as well as sport lessons.

I believe one of the things that made Coach Elmore a great coach was he treated all players and coaches alike. For example, there was one player that smoked which was against the team rules. Coach Elmore was driving around town and spotted the boy stopped at a red light. He was one of our starters and best players. When I got back to school coach called me to his office. He told me that he had seen the boy smoking. He asked me what I thought he should do. You talk about a tough spot! I was in one. I finally said, "You know the weakness in our team. We just do not have many good players." He said, "James I am going to tell you something and I do not want you to forget it. There is not any one player worth breaking the rules for-- now, later, or ever, to satisfy one player." I said, "Thank you coach, I will never forget that." I am just glad it was not me!

We had a pretty good team, but we lost some games that we should have won. We had two players who made All-Conference. That would be Bobby Wood and James Cobb. We played baseball and ran track in the spring. I was not very good at baseball at all. In fact, one of my teammates told me if I could learn how to throw the ball, catch the ball and run I would become a good player. He was one of my best friends. I turned around and said, "Thank you Jimmy Sibley, I like you too." Several years ago, Jimmy was climbing a ladder to clean an upstairs window. His ladder began to fall backward, and Jimmy rode the ladder down to the concrete driveway and hit his head on the concrete. He passed away a few days later, and I really miss him.

That spring, I played baseball until we had a game scheduled one night when I had other plans. My plans were made before Coach Elmore made his schedule. I tried to talk him out of his plans, but he would not change them. I just did not show up for the game. That was a mistake. I went to school the next morning and went down to the dressing room. No uniform in my locker!

I went to the coach's office and Coach Elmore came in. I apologized for not showing up for the game and asked him if I could still be on the track team. He laughed and said, "Yes until you go to another party." I breathed for the first time since seeing my empty locker. We shook hands and he wished me luck in track.

I did three things in track: I ran the mile, half mile, and threw the shot put (the steel ball). We were traveling to our end of the year conference meet and Coach Elmore told me that that I was the only letter earner in track on the team. I never gave up.

One night, my friend Bobby and I were sitting downtown in a Café. (The city of Athens didn't have any restaurants). As we were eating, in walked our friend, Frank Orr. He asked us if we would like to have a summer job. We looked at each other and both said "Yes!". We wanted to know what we would be doing and Frank said that we need people to prepare the chickens to sell at the Sweet Sue Chicken Company. We all three had different jobs. Frank cut up the chickens, Bobby packed the chickens, and I delivered them to the stores and cafes in Athens, Florence, Decatur and Nashville, TN. Sweet Sue paid us 50 cents an hour at the time but that was corrected a year or so later because we were doing business across state lines and the required minimum they could pay was 75 cents per hour. The company sent us the corrected pay retroactively and I got a check on one of my trips back home after I was in college.

Chapter Three

Stories that Changed the Direction of My Life

On June 25, 1950 (a month after I graduated from high school) the war in Korea started. That war changed a lot of young men. They grew into manhood much too fast. I am talking about the ones that went to Korea. We had a National Guard unit in Athens, and people kept talking about the government mobilizing it and sending it to Korea. I had several friends sign up and I began to feel bad about seeing so many of them sign up. I was having trouble going to sleep. Finally, I decided to talk to someone. I talked to my daddy. At first, he did not like the idea and told me so. We sat for a long time and we would talk and then go quiet again. Finally, he told me something I did not know. He told me that he had been in the National Guard as a young man. He said, "If I were in your situation, I more than likely would sign up." The next morning, we went out to the chicken plant and told them we had signed up with the National Guard and we needed to take care of several things and would not be at work anymore. We spent time in our favorite places Athens and tried to say goodbye to our friends. A few days later they put us on a train going to Fort Campbell, Kentucky. We were there six months. It was not too hard or bad, just not too much fun. So, we decided to make our own fun and go see a football game.

The Refrigerator Bowl was played that year in Evansville, Indiana. The Abilene Christian College football team had been chosen to play there. My brother traveled with the team and kept all of the statistics for the team. I really wanted to go to that game but I had several things I had to do to make it happen. First, I had to find out how to get off base and how to get to Evansville, Indiana. To get off the base you had to have a pass and you could get a general every day pass anytime if you were a good boy. You could get off base with a day pass, but you had to be back on base before dark. I paused and thought a little about how I was going to solve this. I had another friend who worked in the office. I saw him one day and he said, "I hear you want to go to a football game." He said, "If you will get me a ticket, I will get you a legal pass off the base." I told him that I would guarantee him a ticket into the ball game. I never gave up.

My next problem was figuring out where we were going to sleep after the game. My friend I was traveling with told me not to worry. Little did I know there was a storm coming up and we watched the game from under the stadium. We got wringing wet and only had our GI clothes that we had worn to the game. Even with all that, after the game I got to go to a room where the Abilene Christian College coaches were and got to meet all five coaches including Coach Morris the basketball coach. We went back to my brother's room to sleep that night in our wet clothes. All five of the coaches that I met there that night were later to become great influences on my life.

The next morning when we got up, all the players and coaches were gone. Our clothes were still wet so I found a dry cleaner and talked to the owner and told him our situation. I told him we could not get on base in these wet clothes. He said to follow him, and he would take care of us. He put us in a room and had us strip down and he put our clothes in the dryer. After they were dry, we were able to get dressed and get out on the highway to hitchhike back to the base. Making the decision to take that trip to see Abilene Christian play football in the Refrigerator Bowl turned out to be one of the best decisions I ever made and ultimately changed the direction of my life. It had a great influence on my life and was a big part of the reason I chose to spend my college days in Abilene, Texas attending Abilene Christian College (now University).

When I got back to the base from the football game, I continued to prepare to be shipped out to Korea to fight in the war. Since I was supposed to go soon, I was required to get a lot of vaccination shots. Two or three days later they said they misplaced my shot information, so I had to have the required shots again. Two or three days after that, they came back and said that I did not have to have the shots after all but they did not explain why. I was confused.

While working on base in the National Guard, I was sent to the place where they were loading equipment that was going to be shipped to Korea - my job was to help load it. After I had worked about half a day, I saw the First Sergeant coming in his jeep. He waved, and I waved back. As it turned out, he was coming to get me to help me clear the base because they were giving me a medical discharge. Apparently, my flat feet did not qualify to go to Korea. There were three others leaving base at the same time. A driver took me close to our house in Athens. I walked into the house and my family and I had a small celebration.

I stayed in Athens 2 or 3 days and got a call from Coach Morris in Abilene. He wanted to know what my plans were for the future. I told him I was thinking about playing basketball with an independent team until fall and then start to college. He said "James, I will make you a deal. If you agree to come to

Abilene tomorrow or the next day, I will guarantee you a 4-year football scholarship and a 4-year basketball scholarship." I said, "How can you afford to do that?" to which he replied, "Well, your brother Bob Cobb and Wally Bullington have already paved the road for you. All you have to do is take the ride." So, I said, "Coach, you made a sale. Now it is my job to see to it that you made the right choice."

The next thing I had to do was break it to my family that I was going to Texas the next morning but it helped that my older brother was already there. My dad took me to the bus station to catch a bus at 1:00 in the morning. He stayed with me outside by the side of the road because the bus station was closed. We had a good talk and then I got on the bus for a 29-hour bus ride that would change my life forever! I never gave up.

We went through Memphis and Little Rock and pulled into Dallas and had a 4-hour layover. Another bus pulled in and I asked the driver where he was going. He said that they were going to Ft. Worth and would be leaving in about 10 minutes.

I asked him if he had room for me. He said yes so, I picked up my bag and changed buses. Come to find out there was another layover in Ft. Worth. I almost gave up. We pulled into the station in Abilene about five o'clock the next morning. I walked into the station and asked someone where I could catch a bus going out to ACC. He said you mean to "The Hill"? When I said yes, he said to go across the street and stand on the corner and I should see a bus pull up that says "The Hill" over the windshield. I rode the bus to the Hill and had no idea where to go. There was a drugstore on one side of the street and a large building on the other. I chose the large building. On the way around the building I met some boys and I stopped one and asked if they would show me to the coaches' building.

One of the boys smiled and said, "Yes I can." You talk about a change in attitude. There was a big one – they seemed to be glad I was there. The boy that was helping me said "Come on, I will show you." I said, "Just show me the way." He took me to a corner and pointed to the building that was the coaches' offices.

I went in and met Coach McClure and we visited a little and he said I looked tired. I told him what I had gone through the last two days. He took me over to the Athletic or "A" dorm and showed me a room and told me that this was my room. I went to bed and slept until Bob (my brother) woke me up about 3:00 in the afternoon. I had shipped some things by bus and since Bob was running the Post Office, he knew when they had come in. He took me back to the "A" dorm. I went to sleep again and then I could hear some other guys talking and wondering who I was. I got up and went to where they had gathered. I told them who I was and why I was there. Well, it looked like things were going to be okay since two of the three boys turned out to be two of my very best friends. That would be Rex Bennett and Bobby Campbell. Rex remained my lifelong friend until he passed away in 2017. I have not heard anything in many years about Bobby Campbell, who became a dentist.

The next day I went over to the gym to watch the team practice. Coach Morris asked me where my uniform was, and

I said that I didn't have one. He called the manager over and told him to take me into the dressing room and give me some shoes and a practice uniform. He got me a ball and I started shooting long shots. He told me to get under the basket and start shooting. He blew the whistle and said, "time for scrimmage." He called Team A then he started calling Team B. He called out 4 players and said Cobb!! I really could not believe it. I quietly said to myself, "Go get 'em!!" I had a lot of fun and played pretty well, especially on defense. I played enough to convince me that I could play. When the semester was over I was getting ready to go home, I saw my friend Wally Bullington coming out the coaches' offices. He stopped me and asked me if I wanted a job this summer. I said "No, I am planning to go home." He said, "What if the job paid $1.75 an hour?" I said, "Where is it and how do we get there? When can we go?" Wally said Coach Beauchamp had a brother-in-law working for Shell Oil and they were looking for 3 or 4 college boys to hire for the summer in Notrees, Texas. It was a small town on the other side of Midland

and Odessa in West Texas (and you are right if you are guessing that there were no trees there).

One Saturday morning Coach Beauchamp loaded up James Lyda, Bill Smith, and me to go to Midland Texas. We went to the Shell Oil office and we signed the papers for the job. We left and went over to Odessa to look for a place to live. We found a place that all 3 of us liked – it was a boarding house. One price covered everything. It covered the room and 3 meals a day. There was one problem though: there wasn't room for all of us. So, we settled it by agreeing for two of us to live in a house next door. We were able to sleep in the house next door, we ate breakfast and dinner at the boarding house and the lady who ran the boarding house fixed us sack lunches every day.

We lived and worked that way all summer, but I did have to take one leave of absence. My father's mother died suddenly. I received a telegram one afternoon when I came in from work. I had sent all my money home. But before I knew it, my buddy James Lyda had gone to every one of the tenants and asked them to loan me some money, so I could get home. He guaranteed that he would pay it back if I could not or would not pay it back. I was able to buy a ticket got to fly back to Alabama as my first time on an airplane. I had used all my money James had given me on the plane ticket so I did not have any money with me on the trip.

The plane stopped at several places, so it took a lot of hours to get to Birmingham. We finally got there, and I realized that I did not have any money to get to my home in Athens. I got off the plane and noticed that the airport had several cars for hire instead of taxis. I took one of the cars and the driver asked me where I was going. I said I needed to go out Highway 31 to the city limits toward Athens so I can hitch a ride home. He looked at me and rolled his eyes and said "ok". He took me to the place and the driver stopped the car and gave me the ticket to pay. I do not remember how much it was. I told him that I was very sorry, but I did not have any money. I do not have any on me for the taxi fee. He said, "Aw, forget it." and went on his way. The cars that came up the road where I was trying to hitch a ride were going very fast. When one car got even with me he blew his horn. He put his brakes on, pulled over, took his hat off and ran to see me. I tried to shake his hand, but he hugged me too tight. It was my boss and great friend that owned the Dr. Pepper plant where I worked for three summers and off and on during the winters. He was happy to take me towards Athens.

As we were going along, we met a car I thought I recognized. The driver blew his horn and stopped. He got out and it was my oldest brother, Luther. I got in and we went to my parents' house. I got cleaned up changed clothes and we went to my grandfather's house. It was almost time for the funeral. Close call!! We went to the funeral. I do not remember the sermon or the songs. I remembered the six boys and girls from the bible school who were my friends in the group.

My brother Bob and I stayed around Athens for a couple of days and then started our journey back to Texas. While I was home, I was trying to come up with enough money to pay back my friends. I was able to send all the money I had to James Lyda by Western Union. I had some happy friends when I got back to Notrees.

There was a summer camp a few miles south of Ft. Worth, Texas where my brother Bob worked that summer. He had his car with him in Alabama so going back to Texas was simple because I rode with him. Hitchhiking from Ft. Worth to Odessa was a picnic compared to trying to hitchhike from Alabama to Texas.

We worked at the plant the rest of the time that summer. There was not very much excitement. James Lyda and I did play softball 3 nights a week. Also, James and I worked out for football until about August 25. We decided we had had enough. We went to the plant and resigned. They said it was ok. I am sad to say that my friend James Lyda has passed away. Rest in peace, James.

James Cobb – ACC Football

Chapter Four

Some Stories from My Time on The Hill (ACC)

It was the fall of 1951 and the beginning of my first full year at Abilene Christian College which was affectionately nicknamed "The Hill" in Abilene, Texas since it was built on one of the few hills in that area. After our summer in Notrees, my friends and I returned to Abilene and checked in with Coach McClure at the coach's office and then went over to our rooms. I had a new roommate who I did not know. His name was Tommy Burleson and was from Oklahoma. When we all graduated from ACC, he moved back to Oklahoma and went to medical school and then practiced medicine for several years.

The other players started coming in and I knew all of them from the previous spring but I was a bit nervous. Fortunately, I got over my nervousness when the guys took me in and made me feel like I was part of the team right away and that helped a lot. I had a surprise at the first practice when Coach Beauchamp called out the defense team and I was on it. We started practicing and I felt like I was doing pretty well until I sprained my ankle. All of this happened four or five days after we started. Needless to say, I was disappointed and did not suit up again until one day before the team left for Des Moines, Iowa for the first game of the season. When practice was over he called all us over and told us he was going to read a list of the players going to the game on the Blue Goose and who was going to travel on the airplane. The Blue Goose was a big oversized car/bus combination with about twelve seats. He called out the name of the ones going on the Blue Goose and I was not on the list. That is one moment in my life that I almost gave up. I am glad I did not give up because very soon he called my name as a rider in the plane. So, I got to ride on the plane to the Des Moines but that wasn't the best part of this story. When we landed, Coach Beauchamp walked back to where I was sitting and said, "James, I am not starting you, but I am going to get you in the game pretty soon. Promise me if you start hurting, you'll please come out." I think one the reasons he had that kind of confidence in me was the fact that I had enrolled in the spring and had gone through most of spring training. We lost the ball game, but I felt like I got off to a good start. Of course, I was trapped a few times and let the runner get away from me a few times. He was an All-American. I was not as good as I wanted to be, but I tried very hard not to give up. The score was 19-7. We were playing three freshmen: Haskel Sinclair, Tommy Morris, and James Cobb. Tommy caught a touchdown pass. We did not have a great season, but we played some good teams. I think our record ended up 6-4.

As soon as football was over we went straight into basketball. We played a few games before we got out for the Christmas holidays. We had one game to play on the day after we got out - that game was somewhere in South Texas. Before we left for the game, Coach Morris called me over to his office. He said, "James, you have been pretty busy. You look like you are tired." To be honest, I was not looking forward to being away from home for the holidays because the team was going to New Mexico to play in a tournament. He asked me, "Why don't you go home for the holidays?" He was right, I was tired and I wanted to go home. I am grateful for a man like Coach Morris who wasn't just about winning ballgames but also about caring for his players. He taught me lessons about leading people that I have used for the rest of my life.

Instead of going back to Abilene from our game in South Texas, I decided to go the bus station in that town and buy a "ticket to daylight" and hitchhike the rest of the way home. We got dressed after the game and I asked Coach to drop me off at the bus station on their way out of town. I walked into the station and went to the ticket window. Coach Morris and the team had already left to go back to Abilene. Now the fun starts. The young man came to the window and asked if he could help me. I said I would like a "ticket to daylight". He said, "I am not familiar with this town." I said, "Oh, I am sorry…Can you look in that book there and tell me where we will be when the sun comes up?

We are going to be going east and if the bus will stop when you see the sun coming up, I will get off the bus. I can pay you now for what you think I will owe you to get to daylight." He did what I asked him to do and I paid him. I thanked him and wondered for a long time how many times he has told that story about the kid who wanted a "ticket to daylight".

I boarded the bus and got off when it was daylight. I found myself on the side of an eastbound highway – the sun was up but the wind was cold as I stood and waited for about two hours to hitch a ride. Finally, a car came by, picked me up, and took me to the west side of New Orleans. I really needed to go to the east side but it was a start. I got out and got on the road again. I had better luck this time finding a ride and I ended up in Athens after a few hours. I stayed about a week and had a great visit with my 3 little sisters and little brother. I spent most of the time with my family and celebrated Christmas with them.

We had a good time, but too soon it was time for me to go to Texas. My dad took me out to the highway going to Memphis.

I caught a ride with three girls and then I got out and got back on the road to catch another ride. A car came by and stopped about 50 yards up the road ahead of me. The driver came running back and asked me where I was going and I told him Dallas. He said, "Well, do you see those two little girls in my car? Do you think you can ride with them?" When I told him about my life as a big brother to three little sisters, he said to get in the car. We rode several hours, and everyone was getting tired and hungry. The man asked me if I was tired and hungry. I said yes. He said, "If you would like, I will pay for a room for you." He did not mention food and I did not either so I went to bed pretty hungry but at least I had a bed. He paid for my room and we all got back on the road the next morning.

We got into Ft. Worth and he dropped me off. A car came by and the driver asked me where I was going. I told him and he said, "Get in." He asked me if I was hungry and I said "a little" even though it had been a couple of days since I had eaten. He stopped at a restaurant and we went in and he said I could have anything on the menu that cost less than 75 cents. I looked and was excited to see that there was a dinner plate for 70 cents. I ate my dinner and thanked him and got back on the road to Abilene where I went back to school. After a few months, basketball and the spring semester were about over. I began to wonder about going to Notrees again. When summer arrived, we had five boys that wanted to go. Coach Beauchamp's brother-in-law worked it out so that we could take all five to work for Shell Oil Company.

I did not know how we would get there, or where we would live when we got there. It was getting close to being time to leave. I decided to take charge since I was the only one that had been there before. I borrowed Rex Bennett's car and went with a friend to Notrees to make arrangements for our group for the summer. We looked around town for a place to live and our foreman asked what we needed. I told him we needed a house that would be good for 5 people. He said he thought he could help. He said, "I have a friend that had to leave for the summer and he had asked me to help him rent the house." The only problem was that there was no furniture in the house. I came up with an idea. What if we were to get furniture out of the dorm? Someone asked how we would get the furniture to Notrees. I said, "Jasper Howard is going with us and he has a Jeepster." There had to be a way to make it work - I was not going to give up.

Saturday came around, school was out, and we needed to load up and go to Notrees. Jasper pulled his Jeepster around and we started loading. We took the furniture out of the dorm and put it in the Jeepster. We had 6 single metal beds, 6 single mattresses, cookware, dishes, silverware, clothes, and 5 men in the Jeepster. Jasper was the driver, Joe Powell next to him, and yours truly next to Joe. It was the three heavy weights in the front seat and the 6 mattresses on the floor of the Jeepster. There was about eighteen inches between the top of the pile and the ceiling of the car. Jerry Mullins volunteered to ride in there. We helped Jerry get settled. He had trouble moving around but he was okay. That left one more to get settled and that would be Tommy

Morris. The Jeepster had a tailgate - something like a pickup truck. He pulled the lid down, turned sideways, pulled his feet up under him, and we got to Notrees without any catastrophes. The only problem we had on the trip was when other cars drove by us, the drivers would almost have a wreck because they were laughing so hard and yelling at us. But we did not give up.

We had a good summer. On Sundays we would go to church and hang around until church was over hoping someone would ask us to go to lunch with them. I would say it worked about half the time. We almost doubled the attendance at church. We had a good time in our household and even though we had some house rules we did have one problem with the food. We had a rule that the person that ate the last bit of food from the food containers should replace it. This rule was not as bad as some of my buddies made it out to be but sometimes they did not follow the rule and we ran out of certain foods. One morning we had a box of cereal in our pantry for breakfast, but we had no milk. We also did not have a refrigerator. We just had an icebox which was filled on occasion with ice when we ordered it to be delivered by the ice man that went to the gas plant. Well, that morning I got the bowls, filled them with cereal and then poured water over in the bowls. When everyone came to the table, they were surprised but managed to eat their cereal anyway. There was nothing left when we finished but it was quite a memorable breakfast. From then on, we made sure we had milk.

At the end of summer, we all left Notrees, went back to school in Abilene and I was to turn in a report about the furniture we had borrowed. We unloaded the furniture and returned everything else to the right place. Surprisingly, there was no damage to anything and I was able to turn in a good report to the school. I do not think they expected that five college guys would be so responsible.

I was glad to start another year on "The Hill" at ACC. My football teammates began to come in and we all reported to the coaches. Being with this group of coaches and players was the greatest thing that had ever happened to me. (I am glad I said that before we were married!) We won the conference championship that year, our coach was named Coach of the Year, and Haskell Sinclair and I made All-Conference along with several other players on the team.

One of the things that my friends and I like to do involved playing pranks. I cannot confirm or deny that I was involved when a cow was found one morning on the second floor of the Administration building but I do know that I thought it was pretty funny. Also, a friend of ours fell asleep one night and a bunch of us tried to move his bed over to the girls' dorm with him sound asleep in it. We were running across campus – I was carrying the back of the bed when the guy on the front part of the bed started making a wide U-turn back to our dorm. I started yelling at him and asking him what he was doing until I realized that we were circling around Dean Adams who was standing there and calmly watching us change our pranking plans that night. He never said a word about it. Then there was the incident of the marbles. We went to chapel everyday in an auditorium with a wooden floor that sloped from back to front. It had the kind of hard wooden seats with metal legs which were attached to the floor. One day in chapel, a bunch of us sat in the back row with some marbles between our feet. When it grew quiet in the auditorium because someone was about to speak, one of us let a marble go and it rolled down the slope, hitting the metal chair legs all the way down – "roll, clink, roll, clink, roll, clink, roll". Then the speaker would try to start again and one of us at the other end of the row would let another marble go from the back row all the way down to the front. It was funny to us and the other students, but not so funny for that speaker!

An older guy on the team, Bob Davidson, tried to give everyone a nickname – especially us newcomers. I was the first one to receive a nickname. When I reported in I was six feet five inches tall. No one on the team (or on campus at the time) was taller than I was. He named me "King Saul," a king in the Bible who was described as being head and shoulders above everyone else. He named Bobby Campbell "Skunk". Please don't ask me why he named him that. He named Ray Hansen "Tiger". I am not entirely sure about the reason I but think it was because he had a way with the girls.

I actually gave the president of ACC, Don Morris, a nickname. One time when were together, I called him Doctor Morris. He called me Doctor Cobb. We did that until I graduated. He was a great man and one of my very good friends. One morning, I was walking across the campus from chapel to the administration building. I saw President Morris coming my way so I waited for him. He came up and invited me to his office for a chat. After we sat down he said, "James, you played a good game Saturday." I said, "Thank you, but if I had played a real good game we might have won." In fact, I believe that comment fits in my "never give up" mantra. Doctor Morris proceeded to say, "if you play as hard as you can for the whole game, you will be okay." I listened to him and tried to do that in every game and in my work. Those wise words have influenced me all of my life. Tommy Morris, I loved your mother and father.

James and Necia – November 26, 1954

Chapter Five

A Love Story that Started with an Apple Core

Every year in the fall at ACC, we celebrated the Homecoming weekend with a big bonfire. Homecoming 1952 was very interesting. Sonny Cleere, Bob Wolfolk and I were walking from the Beanery (campus cafeteria) one night after dinner. We started walking by the girls' dormitory and I said, "Let's go over to the dorm and get 3 girls to go to the bonfire with us." They thought that was a great idea. Sonny had been dating Anita Wood several times and he thought he knew what room she was in and he pointed to a window on the second floor that he thought was hers. That was the way we communicated with the girls. We would throw a small rock to hit the window, the girls would come and raise the window and we would ask them to come downstairs.

Our plan was going really well until Sonny threw his apple core and hit the wrong window. We acted like we had intended to hit that window in the first place. We did not want to admit our mistake, so we invited the girls in that (wrong window) room to save face. There were two girls in the room and we asked them to get another girl and come down and go to the bonfire. They said to wait a few minutes and they would find some else. We said okay and in a few minutes the girl came back to the window and said she could not find anyone else. We asked her to try again. They came back and asked the names of the boys who were with Sonny (Bob and me). The thing that made that night interesting was that Necia (my future wife) was the girl they found to go with us. They told her the names of the three and she about fainted. In the summer before she came from California to Abilene Christian, she had received a school paper and my picture was in it along with two other football players from the deep south -- Alabama and Georgia. She had cut my picture out of the paper and taken it to Abilene Christian with her because I guess she was pretty taken with it. She had decided that she didn't want to meet me unless she was dressed in her best and had her hair done, so she said she absolutely could not go that night. The other girls finally convinced her to come down and she was my date because of a coin flip (see that story in the next paragraph).

We went to the bonfire together and we visited while we were going, while we were there, and while we were coming back. We seemed to have a lot to talk about. I did not have any money and neither did my parents, but I told her that I had grown up on a plantation in the deep south. I was afraid that if she found out that I was poor, and I had a poor family she would not like me. Earlier, Bob and I had flipped the coin to see who would go with Necia. We knew the other girls but did not know her so the loser of the flip was going to be her date. I lost the coin flip and had to go with her. The other boys said, "James, you are hooked." They were right, and I have been happy to be hooked for 63 years.

Photo of James that Necia cut out of the newspaper
July, 1952

Soon after that weekend, I asked her for a date several times and I was a day late every time I asked her. She even turned me down for the football banquet. It was almost our Christmas holidays and we had two basketball games in South Texas. I could not go home to Alabama, so when Bill Johnson asked me to have Christmas with his family in New Mexico, I accepted his invitation. Then when we got back to Abilene and Bill asked me to get a date and double with him and his date, I thought a few minutes and decided to ask Necia. I finally hit the jackpot and the four of us went out to a movie.

After Christmas we played in a basketball tournament. We got third place in the tournament and came back to Abilene before the spring semester started. Before we left for Christmas holidays, Rex Bennett told me to go to his uncle's house in Abilene and get his car to use until he got back to Abilene from his home in Colorado. He was one of the few people in college who owned a car, and his car was a brand-new Pontiac!

I got Rex's car and decided to surprise Necia by visiting her at home. I drove to her family's home which was very close to the campus. I pulled in the driveway and saw Necia through the front window. She got up and ran out of the room because her hair was in rollers. I got out of the car and went to the door. I was welcomed by Necia's dad with more enthusiasm than I had ever experienced before. We had met a few weeks earlier and he was really glad to see me. I went to their house every day after that visit until school started back up for the spring semester. In the fall of 1953, I was honored when Necia said "yes" to my marriage proposal and we made plans for a wedding about a year later.

At the end of the spring semester in 1954, I needed to make a decision about my summer job. It was one of the most difficult decisions I ever had to make. If I went back to Notrees for a fourth summer I would get a nice raise, I would know what I was doing, and I would know the people I was working with and for. After thinking about it for several days, I made a decision. I was going to Denver because coming out of the desert into the mountains just sounded great. My brother Bob lived in Denver, so I had a place to live but I needed to find a job right away. I drove to Denver and went to his place. After visiting a little we got the paper and started looking for help wanted ads. We got on the phone and began trying to set job interview appointments for the next day. We did not have success right away but soon I did get a job as a door to door salesman for a cookware company. On my first morning, I loaded my car with cookware and I set out to work the territory the company had given me. I went to work the next day and the next day with the same results. No sales!!! I made a decision. I was going to try something I had never tried. I was desperate to made a sale - I didn't want to give up.

So, the next morning I got up and went to work, loaded my car and made my first call. I rang the doorbell and this nice lady came to the door and sounded very interested. After I got about one fourth of the sales pitch out, I could tell that she was losing interest. So, I used my new plan. I told her that if she would be willing to keep the cookware, I would give it to her absolutely free of any charges. She slammed the door shut and that was the end of my cookware career.

I left Denver the next day and drove down through Colorado Springs where I stopped to see my friend Rex Bennett. We visited awhile, and he asked me what I was going to do for my summer job. I told him I did not know. He told me that his father-in-law was a very powerful man and could solve problems. When he called his father-in-law, he told Rex to bring me over to him as soon as he could. When we went to see Rex's father-in-law, he told us about a company that was building houses and had some jobs available. Well, this company was starting to build 200 houses on some undeveloped property and the man we spoke with said they were building three houses a week. They were looking to hire men who could rake small rocks and trash off of the yards, so they could sow grass. He told me what the job paid and that I would have to join a union in order to get the job, so I joined my first and last union.

Rex's mother-in-law offered to let me rent a room from them. Their son was in the Army and had been shipped overseas. I accepted the offer and moved in. I reported for work the next morning. I raked rocks and dirt for several weeks. That meant that I and my staff had to finish cleaning three yards every week. One morning my staff finished raking three houses in one day instead of one week. I was so proud of them and I told them so.

One morning soon after that, the supervisor stopped by and chewed me out for standing around too much. I was confused and asked him what he was talking about. He said "every time I came by this morning you were leaning on your rake". I said "That is amazing. I have not used my rake this morning, I have used a shovel." Now this happened the day after my boss, who was my supervisor's boss too, told me that me and my team were doing great. After he chewed me out, I handed him the shovel and said, "Be my guest, I quit right now." He looked shocked and he started backpedaling and telling me to take it easy. He tried to give the shovel back to me, but I would not take it. I went by the office and told them what had happened and where to send my last check.

I went to the home where I was staying and told them goodbye and picked up some money I had paid them in advance for rent. I told everybody goodbye and headed for Abilene. When I got to Abilene I stopped by Necia's parents' house. They told me that she was at the swimming pool. So, I went to the pool and surprised her. She was there with Tommy Morris and his wife. We stayed at the pool a little while and then Necia and I went over to her parents' home. Her parents offered to let me live in the basement until I could move back into the dorm in August. I loved her parents, and especially her mother, who could make the best pies in the world. She made all different kinds of pies and I would always tell her that each one was my favorite – it must have worked because she made me a lot of pies.

I had heard that there was an opening at a service station located in Abilene about a block from the station where I had worked before. I got up the next morning and went over to that station and got the job. I worked there for a few weeks and they had me doing almost everything. I was very busy working the gas pumps in the front, changing oil, and repairing flat tires and washing cars. I did that for a few weeks and one day I looked out the window and saw one of the men I had worked for at the service station where I had worked before. I moved over to work for him the next day. At the new job, all I did was sell gasoline, repair flats of trucks and clean windshields. I worked for him until we had to report for football my senior year.

We decided to have our wedding on the day after Thanksgiving. That would be November 26 and it was also the day after we had our last football game of the season. Necia warned me that she did not want me to get hurt, but if I did, she still expected me to show up at our wedding. We had our wedding in the chapel at the University Church of Christ across the street from ACC. We had a great time. But let's get back to that ball game on the eve of my wedding.

Necia was nervous all through the game. We played as usual but I had problems concentrating on the game which was no surprise to anyone. It became clear to me as the game went along there was no way we could win. We had about 10 minutes left in the game and as one play was running I fell down. I tried to turn over and one of the players had to help me. I had my eyes shut and when he bent over to help me, I winked at him. About that time the students sitting in that section began to start yelling and shouting. Most of them were saying something like, "Oh no, Necia, James is hurt!" She got pretty upset until I got up and she could see that I was fine. It was just a little joke I played on her but it took me many years before I was brave enough to own up to faking my injury that day!!!

I did show up, we did have the wedding and we had lots of friends and family there. We had people from California, Alabama, Oklahoma, and Texas. The wedding was officiated by Necia's great uncle, Tillet S. Teddlie. He was her father's uncle. I had my three sisters, four brothers, and my parents there.

She had her mother, father, brother, her three aunts (Necia's mother's sisters from California), and several cousins there.

Years later I got to spend time with Brother Teddlie on the ACC campus. The library department honored him by creating a special section of the library in his honor. Hundreds of the hymns he wrote, sermons he preached, and books he wrote are in those archives. Then when the school started having "Sing Song," (an annual competition of original choral works with humorous lyrics held every year beginning in 1956) he would come to Abilene and stay with us. I really liked to visit with him and hear how he came to write certain songs. We also went to a program to help him celebrate his 103rd birthday. I think I will look for him when I go to Heaven just as soon as I find Jesus and our families.

After the wedding we left to go to Austin, Texas on our honeymoon. We spent Saturday, Sunday, and Monday in Austin. We went to church on Sunday and saw several friends we knew from school. In fact, one of my very good friends was the preacher that day. A funny thing happened in church. Necia had worn her going away outfit, including her pink hat. When she bowed her head to pray, rice started falling out of her hat onto the floor. Also, we had our first experience eating at the famous Nighthawk restaurant in Austin where we were introduced to rare steak. To this day, we still like our steak rare.

The Newlyweds in Austin – November, 1954

After our honeymoon, we had to return to school. Abilene Christian had several rows of old Army "hutments" that had been moved onto the campus for married students. I had rented one of them for our first home. It was very small — just a little square with one bedroom and a bathroom/shower about the size of a telephone booth. It had a tiny kitchen where we ate our breakfast. Because I was on full scholarship, the school allowed Necia to have one of my three meals each day, so we ate that meal together in the beanery at dinner. This was how we started our life together - from the beginning Necia has been a wonderful partner and supportive cheerleader for me and hopefully I have been the same for her.

Chapter 6

More Sports Stories

I enjoyed my senior year. I must have done something that caused the coaches to put me on the second team at the beginning of the year. I never did find out why they did that. I guess it was they thought they had found someone better than me. Joe Powell, our quarterback went through the same thing except Joe knew why they did it to him. Joe broke his arm just before the last game. We both proved them wrong. Neither of us started the first game but we were both sent in at the end of the first quarter. We both played all of the last three quarters. We did not select team captains for the whole season that year. Instead, the coaches picked the two most valuable players for each game and the ones they picked would serve as captains for the next ball game. After the first game they chose Joe Powell and James Cobb. We both moved to the first team and stayed there the entire season. We were co-captains of the second game when we beat Florida State for the second time. We had another pretty good team. We won six games, tied one, and lost three. I was glad that I did not give up!

Necia and I got married during the few days between football season and basketball season. We came home from our honeymoon on Monday because I had a basketball game on Tuesday in Ft. Worth with TCU. Coach Morris played me the whole game. I made it ok. We had some good players. Instead of going to a basketball tournament in New Mexico, Coach Morris scheduled a trip to Lubbock (Texas Tech), and then down to El Paso (Texas Western) and then to New Mexico (Eastern New Mexico). We did not win many games, but we had fun. Before the season was over, we made an eastern trip. We will talk about that a little later.

At the end of the school year, letter awards were given for athletic performance. An amazing thing happened in my senior year. Three athletes received a total of 28 awards for basketball, football, and track. Tommy Morris got 11 awards, Burl McCoy got 7, and I got 10 awards. That was an all-time record!

In addition to the many athletic awards I received in college, I also was given awards for: "A Club" (men's scholarship award), "Who's Who in American Colleges and Universities," "Trojan Men's Club," and "Lettermen's Club."

We still had one home game before we left on the eastern basketball trip. On that day I received a telegram telling me I had been drafted by the Baltimore Colts NFL professional football team. It said that the head coach (Weeb Ewbank) would be coming to Abilene that day. I had a basketball game that night and would be leaving early the next morning for the eastern trip. I went over to the coaches' office. I walked into the coach's office and said I had a problem. "I got a telegram this morning telling me I have been drafted by the Baltimore Colts. It also said that the head coach would be here sometime today to visit with me." I had a game that night and couldn't meet with him until the game was over.

ACC Football Team 1954

Coach Beauchamp and Coach Jackson both said that they would take care of him until the game was over. When the game was over I showered and found Coach Ewbank. Necia was invited to our meeting, too. We went to the nicest restaurant in Abilene and had dinner and talked. He wanted to know how much money I was expecting. I asked what he had in mind. Coach Beauchamp had told me not to take less than $5,000. When the coach asked me again, I finally said, "If I am worth anything, I am worth $7,500" (never give up!). Coach Eubanks seemed to be okay with that and said that he really liked everything except my weight. He told me that I needed to weigh 10 more pounds before I reported for training camp, and 10 more before the season started.

I tried hard to gain weight but could not seem to gain a single pound. Necia cooked a lot of high calorie and high carb food for me but it didn't seem to help. I drove to the east coast anyway, to the Baltimore Colts' summer training camp in Maryland. I started training and stayed a week. I worked out two times each day and decided I would have a talk with the coach. I went to see the him and told him my problem. Instead of gaining 10 pounds, I had lost another 10 pounds. I did not gain 10 pounds and felt pretty hopeless about gaining 20 or more pounds. I was concerned that all the good coaching jobs would be taken back in Texas and I did not want to be without a job so I decided to leave training camp. I called Necia and told her I was coming home. She wanted to know why, and I said I was too small. She thought that was pretty funny! She had gotten a job teaching school in the Baltimore, MD public school district. She had been hired by mail, so she resigned by mail.

I went back to the room and packed my clothes. One of the other players asked me where I was going and where I lived. I told him, and he asked if he could ride part of the way with me. He lived in a town that was close to my route. I said yes and loaded him up. We went by the bank and cashed some checks that the team had given us for travel expenses. I dropped him off somewhere in Indiana and kept driving to Abilene. I arrived about 9:00pm and went to Necia's parents' house because she had moved in with them. I was really tired after all I had been through and driving across the country so I went straight to bed.

I got up the next morning and had breakfast and visited with the family. They wanted to know everything and had lots of questions. Finally, I went to the coach's office. Another question and answer session but I could tell they were glad to see me. Coach Morris was really glad to see me and he had just gotten a phone call from the Lubbock, TX school system saying they needed a coach who could teach math. He asked me if could teach math. I told him that yes, I was qualified to teach math. "I have the 10 hours of college math that qualifies me." Coach asked me what kind of math I would like to teach. I said plane geometry. Coach asked me if I could go to Lubbock the next morning. I said that we could. He said that he would call the superintendent and tell him that Necia and I would see him in the morning. The superintendent said that he did not have a current opening for Necia, but he would make one.

Graduation 1954

James and Necia

Chapter Seven

Lubbock, Texas

We went to Lubbock the next morning and met with Nat Williams, Superintendent of Lubbock Schools. He welcomed us with open arms and we talked a while and he asked if he could call ACC and get some information on grades. I told him it was ok, so he got up and told us he would be back in a few minutes. He came back and said, "James you have an F in calculus." I said "That is not right – I was supposed to get a withdrawal while passing in that class." Why do I say that? Because I was missing a lot of classes since I was taking frequent basketball and football trips. One day my calculus professor told me I needed to meet with him as I was leaving the room. We met and since I had missed so many classes, I said that I would drop out of the class if he would give me a withdrawal while passing grade when I withdrew. He said he would, so it seemed like he did not hold up his part of the deal. I called the Dean and told him what had happened. The Dean called Mr. Williams and told him he had changed the grade to passing. Mr. Williams told us to report in two weeks and we agreed to do that. We shook hands and departed. We looked at and rented a garage apartment and we both got jobs. Never give up!

My job was Assistant Basketball Coach. Necia's was a second-grade teacher. I would coach the B team and help the varsity coach. We soon found out that the basketball coach was a great man, had a beautiful wife and two young children -- a boy and girl. His name was Max O'Banion. Since we had two weeks before we started our new jobs, we went back to Abilene and left the next day for a trip to California. We had a wonderful trip with Necia's mother, father and Necia's brother, Ervin. It was quite an adventure since there were five of us in a 2-door Ford coupe with no air conditioning, going across the desert in August! Necia's dad rigged up a small fan and a block of ice in the front seat to keep us cool.

Necia grew up in California but after she went to ACC for college, her parents decided to move to Abilene a few months later so this was a trip to visit friends and family they had left behind. We got back to Abilene from our trip to California just in time to go through the graduation exercises for the 1955 graduating class. Then we packed up to move to Lubbock, TX to report for our new jobs.

Mine was teaching four classes of plane geometry, one class of math and one class of study hall at Lubbock High School. These classes were in addition to my coaching jobs for football and basketball. Necia's first teaching job was second grade at George L. Bean Elementary School. We both enjoyed our jobs. We worked for several weeks and decided we needed a better place to live. We found a furnished house and rented it. The only problem was it had four beds and they all fell down and were unusable. The furnished house was close enough for me to walk to school which worked because we only had one car. We needed to move to a house with beds that worked so we moved close to Necia's school and I also worked out a ride with my boss, the head basketball coach, who would take me to and from school so Necia could have the car if she needed it.

We visited the Broadway Church of Christ, and almost immediately found a great couple that encouraged us and became our close friends. They had worked at Abilene Christian and their names were Skipper and Bettye Shipp. They not only introduced us to the people in the church but insisted we place our membership soon. We attended the church and we got involved in several things. They selected me as a Deacon which was very rare because of my age. I was told that I was the youngest deacon to ever be appointed at the Broadway Church of Christ. The minister was Norvel Young, and his wife was Helen, and they were both a great influence for good on our lives. He left Broadway to become the President of Pepperdine University.

When summer came, I began to wonder where I was going to work in the summer, because my pay was only for the 9 months of school. One morning Skipper called me to ask me to come see him. When I got there, he asked me if I would like to sell insurance, I asked him what kind of insurance it was, and he said that it was life insurance. I said, "Skipper, I tried to sell cookware one summer and could not give it away." He told me something I remembered all through years of selling. He said, "James, cookware is sold to help the seller. Insurance is sold to help the buyer." I had never thought about it that way. It made sense to me. I said, "How do we start?" He said, "Come into my office and I will show you." I could not do anything until school was out but when it was out I went to the office of the insurance man. He gave me a little book and some papers. He said to fill out those papers and bring them back to him right away. And that was the beginning of my insurance career....one that would continue for 40 years!

We invited one of my sisters, Joe Ann, who was graduating from high school to come out and live with us. We had told her about Lubbock starting a Christian college. She enrolled there, and was a member of the first graduating class, and the first Homecoming Queen of Lubbock Christian College. She worked several part-time jobs while she was in school and was a member of the Broadway Church with us.

Our first daughter, Cathryn Necia Cobb, was born in Lubbock on September 17, 1958. The morning after she was born, the Lubbock High School principal announced over the loudspeaker that Coach Cobb had a new little cheerleader! Little did he know! Soon after she was born we were shopping for a baby bed, and we found an amazing bed called the "Ducky Bed." When the baby cried, there was a sensor that activated the rocking part of the bed automatically which put her back to sleep and let us sleep, too. She slept in it for many years, and I often thought she might take it to college with her.

We had three different head coaches over the four years I was a coach and teacher at Lubbock High School. Three different head football coaches in four years - unbelievable. After the coach left that was there when I was hired, Coach Moore became head coach. Coach Moore was the football coach at McMurry

University when I was playing at ACC so I enjoyed working with him. Coach Moore brought his own line coach because he was working at his former school with him and because he was a good coach. We worked this way two years and had a lot of success. After that second year of coaching together, Coach Moore was offered a job in south Texas and he took it.

After Coach Moore left, my time as a football coach got a lot more challenging. A new coach was hired to replace him and I do not have very many good memories of that coach. As the new season got started we would win one game and lose two games. Win one and lose two. On one trip back home after playing a game, the coach told me on the way back that he wanted to talk to me. I agreed to talk to him and we met when both of us had an open period at school. He started the conversation by saying that he wanted us to spend all of our time working with the players that were juniors and younger. I said, "Just forget the seniors?" He said "yes". I did not say anything but I made my mind up that moment that I would resign as soon as possible. I did not agree with his strategy and could not support it.

We had our spring game a few weeks later and I had a problem with one of the senior players. He was one of the big senior tackles. When the game was over we noticed we had a football missing. We had separated the seniors from the rest of the team and we knew who had the football. The coach told me to go get it from the big senior tackle. I went over to where they were and asked the boy for the football. He said, "I am keeping it because we won the game." I said, "I am going to count to five and if I do not have that football, I am going to the office and call the police and tell them we have a student who is stealing footballs." He got the ball and tried to hit me with it. I ignored him and joined the other coaches and told the story to them and the head coach laughed. No one else did. He made some remark and said, "Did you catch the pass?" I left without saying anything because I was really upset about the type of leadership this coach was demonstrating. When I got home I told Necia what had happened and what I was going to do. I told her that I was going to quit. I contacted the superintendent and let him know that I was going to quit when school was out. He said, "Why don't you quit now?". It was time to find another job.

That happened on a Monday. The next day on Tuesday, Tommy Morris called me and asked if I would like to have a job. He had worked several months in the insurance business. He had worked for a company that had agencies in Abilene and Lubbock. He told me that the agency in Lubbock was very weak and needed some younger agents. I worked several weeks but could not be satisfied with selling. I sold enough to satisfy the company but not enough to satisfy me. I needed to think about making a change from selling in Lubbock to possibly training agents in Abilene. It was a hard decision because we loved so many things about living in Lubbock. Tommy had told me he might be moving to Waco to work in the home office as head of the training department. He said if he did go to Waco he wanted to tell the company to let me take over his place as an agent trainer in Abilene.

He did and I did. I finally made the decision to move to Abilene. I went to Abilene and started training agents. It turned out to be a great move. Not so much working with the company we had moved with but soon after we moved I had an opportunity to go to work with the company that I would be with for the next 30 years. When Tommy went to Waco, I started servicing his business. We moved to Abilene and rented a house that Tommy's mother had built. The house was very close to the campus and we liked the location. While we lived in the house our second daughter was born.

Cynthia Lynn Cobb was born August 20, 1960. When she was born I had been at the hospital all day and was getting pretty nervous. The nurse finally came out and said, "I am so sorry but you have another baby girl." I almost blew a fuse. I said "Lady, I should hit you. I have been hoping and praying for nine months it would be a girl." The reason I got so upset was when she said she was sorry was because I thought she meant that there was something wrong with Cindy or Necia or both. I was so happy and went to see my daughter and Necia.

When we were living in Abilene, we were quite a distance from my parents and family in Athens, Alabama. We were planning a trip to go see them. We usually made that trip by car, but this time we decided to try out a trip by train. Cathy and Cindy were five and three years old, so it would be nice to have both of us available to take care of them. The dates were set, and my oldest brother, Luther, agreed to pick us up in Memphis, Tennessee and drive us the three hours to Athens.

We boarded the train one afternoon in Abilene, and off we went on our first train trip. We had not been on the train more than a few hours when it made an unscheduled stop. After a long delay, we started up again and then we found out that there had been over twenty train cars attached to our train that were filled with U.S. Army soldiers headed to defend our country during the Cuban Missile Crisis. Needless to say, we were quite relieved to arrive in Memphis and find my brother, Luther, waiting for us. We had a nice visit for a week with my family, and then Luther drove us back to Memphis for our return trip.

We boarded the train late in the day, so the girls could sleep on the way home. About midnight we were all sound asleep, except me. I wasn't feeling well - I seemed to be sick with a cold. I was congested and could not get comfortable. So, when the train stopped in Little Rock, Arkansas to take on some new passengers, I decided to get off of the train, and go into the Train Station to buy a newspaper. I had to go up a flight of stairs to the second floor to get the newspaper. Just as I started down the stairs, the train started to move. In fact, by the time I got to the bottom of the stairs, the train was moving too fast for me to jump on. I started running along beside it and yelling for it to stop. Before I could jump on, it had gone on ahead of me, and I was just running down the tracks behind it. I realized that Necia didn't know where I was, and that I had all of our money and the train tickets in my pocket.

So, I turned around, ran back down the tracks to the station, grabbed a Redcap by the shoulders and yelled, "Where is the next train going to Abilene?" He looked to his left, and said, "Right there, Sir. It's getting ready to leave any minute." I ran to the side, looked in the window, and there were Necia and the girls sound asleep. But the door to get on was on the other side of the train, so I had to run all the way to the back of the train, and to the other side. I jumped on the train just as it started to move, going West to Texas. The train I had chased and tried to catch was the Wrong Train. It was going East, back to Memphis! I sat down, and never moved until we got to Abilene! After I got back on the train to Abilene, I realized there were flights of stairs on four sides of the train station, and I had gotten confused and come down the stairs on the opposite side from where I had gone up. We made many more trips to Athens, Alabama in the years that followed, but all the rest of the trips were taken by car. Taking the train to Memphis no longer seemed like a good idea.

Cindy and Cathy Cobb - Abilene, 1962

Chapter 8

Southwestern Life – Abilene to Oklahoma City

The insurance business in Abilene was going well for me but I still felt like selling was not for me. You see, I was not sold. You had to be sold to sell. My company had offices close to another company called Southwestern Life Insurance Company. I had some health insurance prospects but we did not sell health insurance. So, I went over to the Southwestern offices to see if they could broker a policy. The manager came out and asked if he could help me. I told him why I was there and he gave me all the papers I needed to finish the sale. I took them and started to leave but, on my way out I noticed that they had an empty office. I stopped and asked the manager, "Whose office is that?" Readers, listen closely here because this was a life changing moment for me: "It is yours if you want it." I said, "Are you kidding me?" And he said, "Oh no, I'm not kidding you." Well, I told him that I wanted that office and that is how my long and successful career with Southwestern Life Insurance Company began.

Southwestern Life was founded in 1903 and was still a very strong company. They had a great reputation and had offices all over Texas. I changed over to Southwestern Life. I had to sell one year with them before I could go into management and it was a long year. I learned a lot in that year. One of the things I learned was that my calling was to train new agents--- not to be an agent. When the year was up I was promoted to Sales Supervisor and transferred to Oklahoma City. I thought I had learned a lot in my first year but the truth was that I had not seen anything yet. Before we moved, I drove up to Oklahoma City because I wanted to see the city and find a house for us to buy. We were able to buy a nice house in a neighborhood that had an excellent reputation for it's good schools. Our girls were in the second and fourth grades and they were not too excited to leave their friends in Texas but I knew it was a good move for our family. I bought the house and hoped Necia would like it too. I went back to Abilene and helped everyone get ready to move.

When I was promoted the company furnished me a company car, travel bags, and an expense account. On my trip to buy our house, I stopped by my new office and asked to see the manager. When the manager came out and greeted me, he said, "Where is your hat?" I said, "I do not wear hats. I do not have a hat." He said, "If you work here you do!" Then he said, "Let's go across the street to the back of the store." The hat racks were in the back of the store but I began to think "What have I gotten myself into?" That manager's name was Earl Newton. He asked me what color I liked and I said that I really like blue but the truth was that I had more brown clothes than anything else. I replied, "I will take brown," and Mr. Newton agreed that was good thinking.

After our shopping trip, we went down the street and I realized that I really liked my brown hat. I was thinking (and hoping) that Necia would like it although she has never seen me wear a hat. As we got in Mr. Newton's car he said, "Let's drive to the University of Oklahoma just south of Oklahoma City, in Norman, Oklahoma. I have season football tickets and I think you should too." I told him that I didn't have much money but I would try to come up with money to buy the tickets. He said, "I did not say anything about money. If you listen to me and do what I tell you to do, before you know it you will be buying tickets, dinners, your wife a new car and your girls new bicycles."

A couple of years later I asked him why he treated me so nice that day since he did not really know me. He answered, "James, I talk to men every day. You should see some of them. No, not really. Ugh! I can tell that you are truthful, and I like to have people just like you around me. I know one thing (maybe two). I want us to be a team and I will try to do my best to help you create that team. The other thing is, I will never give up!!" Earl Newton continued to have a positive impact on my career and on my life for many years to come.

One of the many outstanding features of Southwestern Life that we learned about when we lived in Oklahoma City was the wonderful incentive trips that the company offered to its agents for excelling in sales. Necia and I were invited to our first convention in Las Vegas. Neither one of us had ever been to Las Vegas, so we were like two starry-eyed kids. The meeting was held at Caesar's Palace, which had just been built. Through some mix up in reservations, we were given a very large suite to stay in, instead of a regular room. The suite was larger than our house! It had floor to ceiling Roman statues everywhere and was certainly the most luxurious place we had ever seen. Needless to say, we were determined to never miss going on any of Southwestern Life's conventions in the future!

One reason our stay in Oklahoma City was so successful was because we found a wonderful church — Mayfair Church of Christ. Not only did we see people we knew from college but we met a lot of friendly Christians. We were not there very long when we met a lot of people who loved the outdoors and they invited us to go camping with them. We owned nothing that we could use outdoors so we had to go shopping. The first thing we bought was a big tent with a door and windows that was big enough for our family. Then we bought two bunk cots for the girls to sleep on and a foam rubber mattress for Necia and me to sleep on. We also had a butane stove that we could use to cook the food and a lantern for light in the tent. I have great memories of our family camping trips with our friends from church!

Another great experience at church in Oklahoma City was our spiritual growth. I found out that I did not know as much about the Bible as I thought I did. The church had Bible classes before church services. We attended the class every Sunday. When the teacher would say something that we did not think was right, we would go home and check our Bibles. We found out he was right sometimes and sometimes he wasn't. We also found out that we were sometimes right and sometimes we weren't. It encouraged us to read and study the Bible. Another thing we did was drive a church bus on Sunday mornings, Sunday evenings, and Wednesday nights. The bus was called "The Joy Bus." We would do this to pick up children and take them to children's Bible classes and/or church services. Sometimes we would pick up a few parents too. Our girls were big helpers on those bus rides for several months.

Meanwhile, I was enjoying my new position at work. We had a very good life insurance agency and my job was to recruit and train new agents. I liked it and did much better in the training than the recruiting. I left the recruiting to my manager, Mr. Newton. Southwestern Life encouraged all those who were moving "up the ladder" to get a degree called Chartered Life Underwriter (CLU). It was fun for me to take the CLU course. It was designed to be done in five years but I was able to finish in three. I was lucky to pass all the tests (there were A LOT of tests). I spent many hours at night and on weekends studying and working at my manual typewriter. There were no personal computers in 1967. In other words, I did not give up!!

One of the best things about Oklahoma was the time we got to spend on the beautiful lakes there. There was a lake that my manager, Earl Newton liked and another one that I liked. We tried to spend as much time on one as the other because I did not want to get fired. Earl and everyone else liked Lake Tenkiller but I liked Lake Eufaula. One story I remember about the lakes starts with Earl coming by our house one morning to pick me to go to the lake with him. He had his boat with him so I went. When we got to the lake, we got in the boat and went across the lake and as we got to the other side he told me to get into the back of the boat. After he stopped the boat, I noticed him walking back to me carrying some water skies. I thought he wanted me to drive so he could ski. I said "Boss, I do not know how to drive a boat." He said that was okay. "I will be the driver and you will be the water skier." I said, "What?!!! I am not a skier." He said, "I know that but you are going to be one or are you saying that you want to give up?" He had me. I finally said, "Okay, let's go."

I almost had a heart attack while I was trying to learn to ski – remember that I was about 6'5" tall! I tried to get up three times before I made it up and please do not ask me how long I was up. People were standing on the bank of the lake watching us and cheering. This and so many other experiences meant that the three years we spent living in Oklahoma City were some of the best years of our life. I never gave up!

I got up one Monday morning and had a phone call from the home office of Southwestern life in Dallas. It was a message telling me to come to Dallas for a meeting on Tuesday morning. I called the home office and told them I would be there on Tuesday morning. I got up the next morning and drove to Dallas. I had no idea why they called me. I finally got there and walked into the office. I just said, "Here I am." One of the Vice Presidents of Southwestern Life thanked me for coming and he said that they had a problem and wanted me to help them solve it. I said, "Well, let's hear your problem." He said, "We need a new manager in Amarillo, Texas." Now I had been to Amarillo several times and I knew how cold and windy it was. I had to discuss this move with Necia and when I told her about going to Amarillo, she wanted to know if this was my golden city. She was not very excited about moving to Amarillo but she was willing to consider it because of my career. It seemed like the end of the world to her. But soon, she heard a story about Amarillo that changed her mind: "When God was creating the Earth, he was almost finished except for the far west part of Texas. But He was getting very tired so he just decided to smooth that part of it with his hand and go to bed. The next morning God woke up and saw how flat and ugly that part of Texas was, so he made a decision. Because the Texas panhandle was so ugly, he would make sure that the nicest people in the world lived there."

I accepted the offer to move, and one of the toughest things had to do was to tell the bus riders, agents, management team, and Sunday Bible class we were moving to Texas. After we moved, we learned that the story about the people in Amarillo was true and we loved our eight years there!

Chapter 9
Southwestern Life - Amarillo

When we moved to Amarillo we had some challenges with the staff that was there. They were not told they were being replaced before I arrived or maybe they were trying to pull off a big bluff. I tolerated it about three months. I did it by going about my business and not including them. When I had enough of the nonsense, I called the Vice President of production and told him my problem. I also told him that if he did not solve my problem I was going to quit and take all of the good agents with me. He said, "Hold on. I will be there in the morning to take care of it." I told him I wanted the 4 of them gone in 5 days. The group was made up of the former manager, the group manager (he did not think I had the power to move him), and two others. I did not find out what their duties were. I think it was to read the morning paper and drink coffee. He fired all of them in 3 days. That was a load off of my mind and from that point forward things went much better.

A few weeks later an elderly man came into my office and said he was a Southwestern Life policy owner. He said he had heard that I had taken over and wanted to visit a few minutes. I had my secretary bring us a cup of coffee. We talked and visited a while and I asked him if it ever rained there. He said, "Son, every dry spell we have ever had has been broken by a wonderful rain." I had very few conversations about the dry and windy weather after that because it was just a part of living in Amarillo that everyone accepted. In fact, the wind was so powerful in that part of the country that it could be dangerous. One morning I experienced this when I was driving my car to the office in downtown Amarillo. I was moving along slowly and looked out the car window and saw the wind had blown an elderly man down on the sidewalk. I got out of my car asked him if he was hurt bad. I knew he was hurt. I helped him up and he thanked me and said that he was okay. I stayed with him until some of his friends came along to take care of him.

I decided that it was time for some positives in the Amarillo branch. I called for a meeting one morning. I decided we would have an ongoing production contest. I agreed to keep up with production monthly and the winner of the contest would have dinner with Necia and me at the end of each month. The dinner could be in Amarillo or their hometown. It worked very well. It was so good that our agency won the company division award that year. We had five divisions based on size and we were in division number two. We had a meeting at the end of the year and they passed out the awards. I would not accept my award until my two assistants came upon the stage to accept the award with me.

In order to continue to build a strong sales team, I thought of another thing that I would like to try. We had a college in Amarillo and I decided to find one or two college students to let me put them through a program of insurance. I asked among the agents if they knew of anyone that might be interested in finding a job. Someone came by to give me a name and could not say anything bad about David Sharp and his wife. I called them and asked both of them to have dinner with us. David was the only young man that responded to my offer. He was excited about having a job. I explained what I had planned. I wanted him to come to my office every day as soon as school was out and we would spend the rest of the day studying and talking. We did that for about six weeks before school was out.

At that point I told David it was time to talk about a contract. He was ready to talk, and then signed a contract. I let him go out with some of the better agents a few days so he could see how all of the studying and reading and practicing pays off. He worked a few weeks and came in one morning and said, "Boss, can we talk a few minutes?" I asked him what was on his mind. He said, "Boss, I don't think this is for me. I don't believe I can sell insurance." I said, "I am glad you used the word "believe" because it is hard to fight the word "can't".

As long as you don't give up, you will have a chance. I want you to remember two things. Number one, I am here to fight for you. Number two, change your thoughts to positive thoughts. Do it with everything you think about - not just what we are doing, but everything. I said I would help you and I will start now. We have been paying you three hundred and fifty dollars a month. We are changing that today to four-hundred a month right now if you stay." He looked at me and could not believe what he had just heard. This happened in 1974 and David is still in the life insurance business in San Angelo, Texas today. He did not give up!!!!

We had many good successes in Amarillo, and of course the challenging times as well. One of the best things that happened to me personally was that I was named National Manager of the Year. I think I was able to achieve that level of success because I never gave up. We lived in Amarillo eight years, and all of us have good memories of living there. Both daughters graduated from Tascosa High School.

Necia will tell you that one of her greatest wishes came true in Amarillo. For as long as she could remember, she wanted to take a trip to Hawaii. She had grown up in California watching "Hilo Hattie," one of the first television programs. It just so happened that the first convention that I could qualify for after we moved to Amarillo was a trip to Hawaii. We had not been in Amarillo very long, and I really didn't want to talk about it with Necia, because the agency production level that it would take for us to be invited was way above anything the Amarillo agency had ever produced. She says that one of the best days of her life was when I came home and handed her a beautiful brochure of the Sheraton Waikiki and asked her if she would like to go to Honolulu. It really was a dream come true for her! Little did either one of us dream that we would make 26 trips to Hawaii over the next 30 years!!!

Just like in the other places we lived, we loved the church we became a part of. We went to church with several friends from college. First of all, we had Bob Barnhill the minister of the

Central Church of Christ. We had a few members like Warlick Thomas who I played basketball with, and Bill Johnson was another one. I am sorry to say that Bill has passed away and if there is a heaven Bill is there. He was one of the best friends and one of the best Christians I have ever known. God bless you Bill and save me a seat. Our Sunday school class teacher was our dear friend Ron Willingham. When they asked Ron to teach he asked me to be the class leader and if anyone disagreed with him to get up and take them outside. Of course, he was kidding (I think). One Sunday, the minister came in and stayed for class. I never did know why he was there. I told Ron he was checking to see if we were using the Bible in our study.

When we moved to Amarillo we could not find a house we wanted to buy, so we rented an apartment for 3 months in the summer, which pleased Cathy and Cindy because there was a swimming pool. They enrolled in school- Cathy in junior high school (7th grade) and Cindy in the fifth grade in Elementary School. They liked the school, the teachers, and made many new friends. Just before school started we found a beautiful house to buy, which was in walking distance of both schools. That summer I decided I would learn how to play golf. I did not take lessons but I just played and practiced. I was not very good but I was good enough to play with some of my friends. That was my goal and I never gave up.

Necia decided she wanted to learn how to play golf also. She took lessons and practiced and could play very well. We played with Dan and Joann Flemming every Sunday afternoon at Tascosa Country Club. They were a great couple and had two wonderful children, Larry and Linda. I am sorry to say that Joann, Dan, and their son have all passed away.

Cathy and Cindy wanted to be athletes. Cindy was on the track team as a long jumper. She did very well and enjoyed it. Cathy chose golf and was on the golf team all 3 years of high school. They had a good team and I watched every game they played. I got called out by one of the mothers of a player on one of the teams we played. She said that I was telling Cathy what to do on every hole. There was no truth in the statement. Actually, if she had said Cathy was helping me. it would have been closer to the truth.

Things began to speed up the last few months we were in Amarillo. In September of 1976 Cathy enrolled in Abilene Christian University (ACU). Cindy was a junior in High School. In September 1977 Cindy started her senior year and graduated in January of 1978. In September of 1978, Cathy and Cindy both went to ACU. Cathy graduated in 1980 with a degree in Business Marketing. Cindy transferred to the University of Texas in Arlington and graduated in 1983 with a degree in Architecture. About this time the company transferred me to Ft. Worth and promoted me to Regional Vice President.

1980, Ft Worth, TX - Cobb family
(Cathy married Jack Rosenquist)

Chapter 10

Southwestern Life – Ft Worth and Dallas

The Fort Worth agency was one of the largest Southwestern Life agencies in the country, but in recent years it had stopped growing because the manager and some of the agents were getting older, and not producing the business they had done in the past. To avoid problems with getting a new manager (me), the company set up a new sub agency in one of the suburbs and moved the existing Ft Worth management out of the Ft Worth agency to that sub agency.

Then I was able to step into the role as Manager of the Ft Worth agency and started building and growing that group to a successful agency again for SWL. I was in good health, but my new doctor in Fort Worth strongly suggested that I should get involved in some type of physical activity every day. So, I decided to start a running program early every morning before I got ready for work. Necia decided to join me, and we ran together every morning for many years. We also enjoyed participating in 10K races on some Saturdays.

We continued to enjoy the company trips and meetings, and we were fortunate enough to be invited to all the conventions all over the world for many years. While I was working in Ft. Worth, we qualified to attend the Southwestern Life trip to Hong Kong and Thailand (Bangkok and Chiang Mai). It was an amazing trip, and we got to see parts of the world that neither one of us had ever seen. After managing the Ft. Worth agency for a couple of years, the company promoted me to Executive Vice President of National Production, and I started working out of the corporate offices in downtown Dallas. We continued to live in Ft. Worth, and I had about a 30-minute commute every day. It was a very interesting time in my career. I was able to travel all over the U.S., hiring managers, and setting up company agencies in many cities and states. One of my job descriptions was to plan the Southwestern Life Incentive Trips. So, during my thirty-year career, Necia and I were privileged to travel to the Hawaiian Islands of Maui, Oahu, Big Island, Kauai, Lanai, and Molokai. We also went to Tahiti, Bora Bora, Switzerland, Canada, Rome and Florence, Italy. We also travelled to most of the Virgin Islands in the Caribbean. We went to Bermuda, Austria, France, and Monaco. We felt truly blessed to get to see so much of the world. It was beyond our wildest dreams and I was glad that I did not give up.

Many changes were happening in the life insurance business and Southwestern Life was sold to a company in Pennsylvania. We never knew what was going to happen from one day to the next. The decision was made to physically move Southwestern Life to Philadelphia. So, several of the managers and corporate executives started selling their homes and making arrangements to move to Philadelphia. After this decision had been in effect for a few months, the new owners decided that was a bad decision, and asked everyone to stay in Dallas, and the Philadelphia company was moved to Dallas.

The new company appointed a new president who did not know the staff at Southwestern Life and he started replacing people. He made me fire the man that had been responsible for my working for Southwestern Life in the first place, in Abilene. That man helped me get my first promotion and start my climb up the corporate ladder. It was one of the most difficult tasks I have ever had to do. I decided it was time to play my last ace and find out if I was going to be keeping my job or not. One day I asked the new president to have dinner with Necia and me that night. I said I knew a good restaurant and asked him to bring his wife. He said she had not moved to Dallas yet. I called my good friend and asked him to meet us at the restaurant 30 minutes after we started dinner. Necia and I arrived and the president was already there. We got a table for four and sat down. My friend walked in I said, "Oh my, I need to meet with him for a few minutes." I suggested that the president and Necia visit while I took care of some business with my friend. Everybody agreed that was a good thing and after an hour and thirty minutes we got back together. While I was gone, the president gave Necia a test about me. She must have done a good job because it lasted a long time. As we got ready to leave the restaurant, he came over and shook my hand and said, "Thank you. Your wife just saved me from making one of the biggest mistakes I could've ever made." My wife helped me keep my job – she was my ace.

In this time of stress and uncertainty, Necia and I got to a point where she thought I was ruining my health. We both had enough to worry about (my health, my job, the future of my company, etc.) but we had not seen anything yet. It was December of 1986 and we found out that Necia had breast cancer. So, now we had a much bigger problem to worry about. As I look back, I am grateful we had a great doctor in Dallas. She had breast surgery and mastectomy followed by several months of chemotherapy. She did really well until she went in for her 5-year checkup. Then the breast cancer was diagnosed on the other side, so she had a second mastectomy. I am proud that she is a survivor and grateful to God that she made it through some very serious health challenges.

Sometime in early March I decided that I was ready for a change. I would be 55 on March 15. I could retire and continue my salary for one year, keep my health insurance as long as Necia or I lived, plus I had a bonus based on the 1986 production and a lifetime pension. I walked into the new company owners' office and said, "I am going to retire on March 31." He looked at me with shock and dismay. He would have no one to help him take over. He asked me why I was leaving. I said, "I know how this works. If I stay, nothing that we just talked about will happen. My assistant will take over my job at the same salary he has, but without any bonuses." That was exactly how it worked out, but the company went out of business in less than two years. Please do not jump to conclusions. I could not have saved the company because the new owners did not have the honesty and integrity that Southwestern Life had always been founded on. I wanted to retire while my own reputation was still intact, as well as my health. So, I moved on and have had many other adventures since I retired – I even enjoyed a few more careers but those stories will have to wait until my next book.

I have really enjoyed sharing the first 55 years of my life with you! It was a wonderful first half. I'm well into the second half, and it has also been great. God has blessed our family beyond measure. We live in Dallas, Texas now. Our devoted family has grown from four to ten. The names of our immediate family members are: Cathy and Jack Rosenquist, Amy Rosenquist, James, Elaina, and baby Jack Rosenquist, Cindy and Jim Foege.

God bless you and all those you love — and Never Give Up!

57762668R00072

Made in the USA
Columbia, SC
17 May 2019